UNEⓍPLAINED

STRANGE ANIMALS

Rupert Matthews

QED

Project Editor: Paul Manning/White-Thomson Publishing
Designer: Tim Mayer/White-Thomson Publishing
Picture Researcher: Maria Joannou

First published in the UK in 2010 by
QED Publishing
A Quarto Group Company
226 City Road
London EC1V 2TT

www.qed-publishing.co.uk

ISBN 978-1-84835-440-1

Printed in China

Picture credits
Key: t=top, b=bottom, r=right, l=left, c=centre

Corbis Wayne Lawler/Ecoscene 11, Vo 17t, Trung Dung,
Reuters 29t; **Getty Images** Aurora/Robert Caputo 23;
Photolibrary Cusp/Peter Adams 15, John Warburton-Lee
Photography/Nigel Pavitt 27; **Rex Features** Everett Collection
2, 4t, 16; **Science Photo Library** Tom Mchugh 14, Joe Tucciarone
22b, 31; **Shutterstock** Clay Chan 1, Joe Gough 5t, Richard Fitzer
7t, Natalia Bratslavsky 8b, Andrej Pol 13b, Jeff Banke 17b, Ralf
Juergen Kraft 18, Lijuah Guo 19, almondd 21t, Stephen Mulcahey
24b, Christopher Meder – Photography 25b, Adrian Phillips 28;
Topham Picturepoint 4b, 9, 20, 22t, 25t, 29t, Fortean/Healy 5,
7b, Fortean/Richard Svensson 6, Fortean 8t, 24t, 26; **Wikimedia
Commons** 12, 21b, Dmitry Bogdanov 10, Department of Defense/
US Navy 13t.

The words in bold are explained in
the Glossary on page 30.

You can find the answers
to the questions asked on
these notebooks on page 31.

CONTENTS

WHAT IS A CRYPTID?

For centuries, people have told stories of strange, often scary creatures that do not seem to belong to any known **species**. These animals are called **cryptids**, or 'hidden ones'. But how do we know whether or not a cryptid really exists?

The Loch Ness monster is one of the most famous cryptids of all time. This picture first appeared in 1934, but was later found to be a fake.

INVESTIGATING CRYPTIDS

Many of the stories about cryptids come from ancient myths and legends. But some people claim to have taken photos and videos of cryptids – and even collected evidence of them, such as footprints, droppings and fur. Of course, none of this proves that a cryptid really exists. Some of the evidence has been shown to be fake – but not all of it...

This footprint photographed in 1951 is said to be that of a Yeti, a giant ape-like creature believed by some to live in the mountains of Nepal.

CRYPTID HUNTERS

Often the evidence for cryptids is strong. But scientists will not say that a cryptid really exists until it has been captured and studied in a laboratory.

A person who searches for cryptids is called a **cryptozoologist**, which means 'a person who studies hidden animals'. People who search for cryptids often need to travel to far-off parts of the world. They must know how to survive in jungles, forests, mountains and other harsh environments.

Cryptids are often confused with animals that belong to known species. This hand skeleton was said to belong to a Yeti, but was later found to be that of a bear.

COLLECTING EVIDENCE

Among the tools used by cryptid hunters are:

Camera	To take photos and movies.
Plaster	To take casts of footprints.
Plastic bags	To collect and store evidence such as hairs, droppings, etc.
Traps	To catch cryptids for future study.
Maps and notebooks	To record the time and place of sightings.

How would you feel if you came across mysterious footprints on a mountainside, or saw a giant creature coming towards you through the snow?

CRYPTID FILE

Subject	Yeti
Height	About 1.6 metres
Habitat	Himalayan mountains
Status	UNEXPLAINED

IN SEARCH OF THE YETI

In the late nineteenth century, travellers to Nepal and Tibet began to hear stories of a huge ape-like creature that lived deep in the Himalayan mountains. Local people called it the 'Yeti', or 'animal of the rocks'. The creature was said to be very strong, but it was shy and usually ran off when it saw humans.

In 1951, Eric Shipton, a well-known British mountaineer, was on a climbing trip in Nepal when he saw strange footprints, which his guide told him were made by the Yeti. Shipton followed the tracks and took photos of them. His pictures were later published all over the world.

 Many climbers and local people claim to have seen the Yeti hunting for food in the mountains. Some even claim to have captured the creature on film.

STRANGE CRIES

One person who claims to have actually seen the Yeti is British mountaineer Don Whillans. During an **expedition** to the Himalayas in 1970, Whillans was looking for a place to pitch his tent when he heard strange cries. Later that night, he saw a large shape moving in the darkness outside. The next day, he found footprints and spent 20 minutes watching through binoculars as a large, ape-like creature searched for food not far from his camp.

This animal **scalp** is believed to belong to a Yeti. It is kept by monks at Kumjung **monastery**, high in the Himalayan mountains.

FACT OR FAKE?

The most recent sighting of Yeti footprints was by US TV presenter Josh Gates in December 2007. Gates found a huge five-toed pawmark 33 centimetres long and 25 wide. Two heelprints were also found. An expert who examined the prints was convinced they were genuine.

How tall is the Yeti believed to be?

Who first took photos of Yeti footprints?

Which climber claims to have seen the Yeti?

IN SEARCH OF BIGFOOT

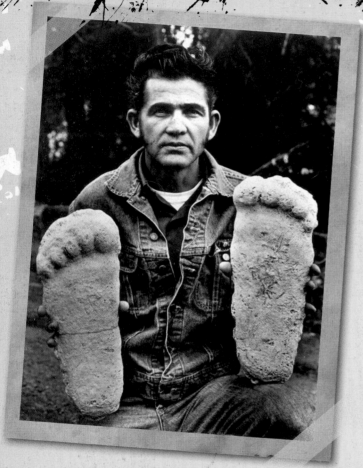

Cryptid hunter Robert Gimlin holds plaster casts made from footprints found at Bluff Creek, California, in 1967.

If you go down to the woods today... watch out for **Bigfoot!** More than 300 people claim to have seen this fearsome creature in the remote forests of the northwest USA.

THE BIGFOOT TRAIL

In 1958, workmen were building a road in Bluff Creek, a remote part of northern California, when they found mysterious footprints made by a creature that they nicknamed 'Bigfoot'. The reports made headlines across the USA, and Bigfoot became famous. But could Bigfoot really exist? In 1967, investigators Roger Patterson and Robert Gimlin decided to visit Bluff Creek to find out.

Dense forest like this still covers vast areas of the American northwest.

What is the Native American name for Bigfoot?

How heavy is Bigfoot said to be?

Who claimed to have filmed Bigfoot in 1967?

Native Americans often used to tell stories about a powerful ape-like animal that lived in the woods. Could this be the creature they called 'Sasquatch'?

CRYPTID FILE

Subject	Bigfoot
Height	2.4 metres
Weight	220 kilograms
Habitat	Northwest USA
Status	UNEXPLAINED

BIGFOOT THE MOVIE

After two weeks of searching, Patterson and Gimlin were riding up a narrow creek when they saw a huge ape-like animal about 25 metres away. Patterson's horse was alarmed and reared up, throwing him from the saddle. Soon Patterson was back on his feet and filmed the creature as it walked away into the woods.

Patterson's film of Bigfoot caused huge debate. Patterson swore on his deathbed that the film was genuine. Gimlin also believes that what the two men saw was the North American Bigfoot.

FACT OR FAKE?

The Patterson film has been examined many times by experts. Some scientists say that there is no such thing as Bigfoot and that the 'creature' in the film is just a man in an ape-suit. Others claim it would be impossible for an actor to fake the muscle movements that the creature makes in the film.

Before the first European settlers arrived in Australia in 1788, 'Terra Australis' was thought to be full of bizarre and terrifying creatures – and none was more frightening than the **Bunyip**!

FEROCIOUS

The first reports of the Bunyip came from **Aboriginal** tribesmen. They warned settlers to watch out for a **ferocious** seal-like creature about 9 metres long that lived in lakes and lagoons and attacked anyone who came near.

CRYPTID FILE

Subject	Bunyip
Size	About 9 metres long
Habitat	Southeast Australia
Status	EXPLAINED!

Some experts believe that Bunyips were really giant marsupials known as diprotodons. Diprotodons lived about 1.6 million years ago. Their bones have been found in many places across Australia.

STRANGE SOUNDS

Between 1840 and 1850, several settlers reported seeing strange **amphibious** creatures. Unusual bones were found buried in the mud of lakes and rivers. Suddenly, people all over the country were talking about Bunyips. Many claimed to have heard strange sounds coming from the lagoons at night.

According to one theory, the Bunyip was a type of seal that had strayed far from the coast and had gradually **adapted** to life in rivers and lagoons..

FACT OR FAKE?

In 1846, a skull believed to be that of a Bunyip was found on the banks of the Murrumbidgee River in New South Wales and put on display in a museum in Sydney. However, a scientist who examined it decided that it belonged to a deformed foal, and was not evidence of a new species.

WHAT HAPPENED NEXT?

By the 1880s, experts began to realize that the old stories told by the Aborigines were about a mythical beast, not a real creature. Some of the bones found in old lakes were identified as belonging to a **prehistoric** giant wombat called the diprotodon. Real Bunyips probably never existed — but stories about them are still part of Australian folklore to this day.

How did the first settlers hear about the Bunyip?

Where were Bunyips believed to live?

Where was the skull of a Bunyip said to have been found in 1846?

11

SEA MONSTER AHOY!

Ever since ships have sailed the seas, sailors have been spinning tales about fantastic sea creatures. Most are probably untrue, or at least exaggerated. But some cannot be explained quite so easily....

TERRIBLE CREATURE

An early recorded sighting of a sea monster was by a Scandinavian missionary, Hans Egede. On 6 July 1734, Egede's ship was sailing past the coast of Greenland when suddenly all on board "saw a most terrible creature, resembling nothing they had ever seen before".

Egede wrote: "The monster lifted its head higher than the crow's nest on the main mast. Giant fins propelled it through the water. Later the sailors saw its tail as well. The monster was longer than our whole ship."

 This scene is imaginary, but the giant squid pictured here is a real creature that is found in many of the world's oceans.

US servicemen display a giant oarfish found on the shores of the Pacific. In the past, oarfish have often been mistaken for sea serpents. They are a recognized species, but very rare.

THE DAEDALUS SIGHTING

On 6 August 1848, the British warship HMS *Daedalus* was cruising in the South Atlantic, when the duty officer spotted what looked like a giant sea snake in the water. For 20 minutes, everybody on board watched the serpent moving through the sea with its oval-shaped head poking out of the water.

Later, Captain M'Quhae of the *Daedalus* wrote a report of the sighting. Scientists did not believe the story, but the captain insisted that every word was true.

CRYPTID FILE

Subject	Sea serpent
Length	20 metres
Sighting	In oceans worldwide
Status	UNEXPLAINED

FACT OR FAKE?

Because the oceans are so vast, it is possible that large creatures may be living there undetected. In 2003, a US cryptozoologist examined all the evidence for sea cryptids. He suggested that the oceans might contain up to 10 types of large creature that do not belong to any known species.

Who saw a sea serpent in 1734?

Where did the sighting take place?

How long was the serpent?

THE MAPINGUARI

Long ago in the tropical rainforests of Brazil and Bolivia, people told of a **sloth**-like creature with a terrible cry — and an even more terrible smell. Meet the Mapinguari!

Locals describe the Mapinguari as being about 2.5 metres tall, covered in red fur, foul-smelling and with claws strong enough to rip apart a fully grown palm tree.

CRYPTID FILE

Subject Mapinguari
Height About 2.5 metres
Habitat South America
Status UNEXPLAINED

CLAWED ANIMAL

In 1888, Ramón Lista, the governor of Santa Cruz Province in Argentina, was out hunting when he suddenly saw a huge clawed animal rearing up on its hind legs in front of him. Terrified, Lista shot at it — but missed. While Lista reloaded his gun, the animal walked away into the scrubland.

THE MYLODON

Later, Lista told his friend, zoologist Florentino Ameghino, about his experience. From his description, Ameghino soon realized that the creature was almost identical to the Mylodon, a type of giant sloth that was thought to have died out centuries before.

Two years later, a 'big game' hunter called Vernon Hesketh-Prichard set out for Patagonia to shoot a 'Mapinguari' and bring it back for study. Despite travelling for over 1500 kilometres through the forests and grasslands of Patagonia, Hesketh-Prichard eventually gave up his quest and returned empty-handed.

FACT OR FAKE?

Most of the sightings of the Mapinguari took place more than 250 years ago, but many people believe that the creature still exists. The ornithologist David Oren has searched for the Mapinguari for many years. However, none of the evidence he has found has convinced the experts.

In his search for the Mapinguari, the hunter and explorer Vernon Hesketh-Prichard travelled huge distances across these grasslands in Patagonia in the southernmost part of South America.

Who shot at a Mapinguari in 1888?

How tall is the Mapinguari said to be?

Who travelled for 1500 kilometres in search of a Mapinguari?

The Loch Ness monster is probably the most famous cryptid in the world. Nobody has ever proved that 'Nessie' really exists – but lots of people would certainly like the stories to be true!

CRYPTID FILE

Subject	The Loch Ness monster
Length	About 8 metres
Habitat	Loch Ness, Scotland
Status	UNEXPLAINED

LEGENDS OF THE MONSTER

Stories and legends of the Loch Ness monster go back as far as 570 CE. For a long time, the creature was hardly known outside Scotland. But when a new road was built along the side of Loch Ness in the 1930s, many more people came to visit the area – and Nessie's fame began to spread.

EXTRAORDINARY

On 22 July 1933, a Londoner, George Spicer, and his wife were driving beside the loch when they saw "a most extraordinary form of animal" lurch across the road, leaving a trail of broken undergrowth behind it. Spicer reported the sighting to the local paper. Soon 'Loch Ness monster' stories were all over the national press.

This photograph taken in 1934 is one of the best known images of Nessie. Unlike other pictures, it shows the creature's head and neck. The image was revealed as a hoax in 1994.

FACT OR FAKE?

Over the years many scientists have tried to find out if the Loch Ness monster really exists. One of the most thorough investigations was by the BBC in 2003, when scientists used special equipment to search the loch for unusual sounds. They found no evidence of anything bigger than a fish.

Where is Loch Ness?

Who saw the monster in 1933?

When did the BBC carry out an investigation?

Alex Campbell lived and worked for many years in the Loch Ness area. He claimed to have seen the monster 18 times.

SPECTACLE ON LOCH NESS

What was it?

(A CORRESPONDENT).

...for generations been credited home of a fearsome-looking ...somehow or other, the "water-...legendary creature is called, has ...garded as a myth, if not a joke. ...rom in the news that the beast ...once more, for, on Friday of last ...known business man, who lives ...and his wife in University

CAUGHT ON CAMERA

Since the 1930s, several people claim to have photographed a serpent-like creature swimming with its head above the water. But the evidence has never convinced the experts.

One theory is that Nessie could be related to a creature known as a plesiosaur, which might have been trapped in the loch at the end of the last Ice Age. However, experts argue that all known plesiosaurs died out millions of years before Loch Ness was formed.

Loch Ness was formed in the last Ice Age. One of Scotland's deepest lochs, it contains as much water as all the lakes of England and Wales put together.

Long before the first European **settlers** came to the shores of Lake Okanagan in Canada, local people told stories of Ogopogo, a terrible monster living deep in the lake.

Many believe that the Ogopogo is a plesiosaur, a giant animal that lived in the sea millions of years ago. The name 'Ogopogo' comes from a Native American song.

CRYPTID FILE

Name	Ogopogo
Length	Up to 20 metres
Habitat	Lake Okanagan, British Columbia, Canada
Status	UNEXPLAINED

A HUGE CREATURE

On 8 July 1952, two friends were sitting beside Lake Okanagan when they saw a huge creature in the water about 85 metres away. Its body was long and thin, with a horse-like head on a long neck. For three minutes, the two women watched in amazement as it splashed around in the lake before diving out of sight.

The next day, they reported the sighting to the local newspaper. Soon dozens of other people were writing in to report their own sightings.

Lake Okanagan is 135 kilometres long and certainly deep enough to contain a large creature. There are towns and villages on the shore of the lake, but the area around it is mostly forested and few people live there.

VANISHED

Researchers who investigated the story found there had been many mysterious incidents in the lake over the years. Swimmers had vanished; boats had been attacked. Horses tethered to canoes had been dragged underwater by an unknown force. Sometimes a large creature had even been seen rising up from the lake to grab birds in mid-air.

SIGHTINGS

The sightings have continued right up to the present day. Six times a year, on average, someone reports seeing the creature. Many people claim to have photographed and filmed Ogopogo, but so far no one has ever proved the creature really exists.

FACT OR FAKE?

Ogopogo was first seen by people as long ago as the 1800s. In 1926, a large group of people in cars parked on the shore of the lake all said that they saw the creature at the same time. A local newspaper editor wrote: "Too many reputable people have seen the monster to ignore the seriousness of the actual facts."

How big is Ogopogo said to be?

Where does the name Ogopogo come from?

Where is Ogopogo said to live?

THE ORANG PENDEK

In central Sumatra, Indonesia, a strange half-human creature is said to live in the jungle. Villagers fear it. But some believe the 'Orang Pendek' could hold the key to one of the great mysteries of evolution.

Eyewitnesses say that the Orang Pendek looks like a small, hairy human being. It has a human nose and shoulder-length hair, and gives a low whistle-like call.

SUPERSTITION

When British naturalist Debbie Martyr heard about an 'ape-man' living in the jungle of central Sumatra, she put the stories down to local superstition. But in 1989, she had an experience that changed her life forever: she saw the creature with her own eyes!

"It was a gorgeous colour, walking upright" Debbie said. "It didn't look like anything I had seen in books or zoos. I had a camera in my hand at the time, but I dropped it, I was so shocked."

FACT OR FAKE?

One theory is that the Orang Pendek could be a survivor from a 'missing stage' of evolution, when apes first began to learn to walk upright like human beings. But is the Orang Pendek an animal – or a human? Until more evidence is found, no one can say.

EVIDENCE

Determined to find the truth behind the Orang Pendek stories, Debbie set out to collect as much evidence as she could. With a photographer, she travelled hundreds of miles through the jungle in the hope of seeing the creature again.

After 15 years, Debbie finally gave up her search. But deep in the Sumatran jungle, others are now carrying on the work that she began.

Apes such as this orangutan walk mostly on all fours, but the creature seen by Debbie Martyr walked upright like a human being.

CRYPTID FILE

Name Orang Pendek
Height About 1 metre
Habitat Sumatra, Indonesia
Status UNEXPLAINED

How tall is the Orang Pendek?

Where is the creature said to live?

Who spent 15 years collecting evidence about the Orang Pendek?

THE LAST DINOSAUR

Imagine travelling in central Africa and coming across a creature as scary as the Mokele-Mbembe! You would certainly want to tell your friends about it. But would they believe you?

'ONE WHO STOPS RIVERS'

In February 1932, the Scottish naturalist Ivan Sanderson was travelling along the Mainyu River in west Africa when he saw a huge dinosaur-like creature on the bank. Within moments it disappeared into the water. According to his guides, it was called Mokele-Mbembe – literally, 'one who stops rivers' – and had been part of local folklore for centuries.

The naturalist and writer Ivan Sanderson made many journeys to Africa in search of rare and unusual animals.

Mokele-Mbembe was said to be between the size of an elephant and a hippopotamus. It had a long neck and tail and round clawed feet like a dinosaur.

CRYPTID FILE

Name	Mokele-Mbembe
Size	Up to 20 metres long
Habitat	Congo Basin, Central Africa
Status	EXPLAINED

These mangrove swamps near the mouth of the Congo River have often been thought to be inhabited by strange dinosaur-like creatures.

THE SEARCH GOES ON

After Sanderson's sighting, others set out to find Mokele-Mbembe. In 1981, two US cryptid hunters, Roy Mackal and Jack Bryan, were travelling down the Congo River when they heard a loud splash and saw something in the water. Both men claim that it was "much bigger than either a crocodile or a hippo". Some explorers claim to have filmed the creature, but most of the evidence has turned out to be fake.

Could there be a large dinosaur-like creature hiding somewhere in the rivers of Central Africa? It seems unlikely. Most experts now believe that Mokele-Mbembe only ever existed in **legend**.

FACT OR FAKE?

In 1919, a 32-man team of explorers and scientists set out for central Africa in search of new plants and animals. During the expedition, the team's African guides found large, unexplained tracks along the bank of a river . Later they heard mysterious roars coming from a swamp that were unlike those of any known animal.

Where is the Mokele-Mbembe said to live?

What does 'Mokele-Mbembe' mean?

Who claimed to have seen Mokele-Mbembe in 1932?

23

CRYPTID FILE

Name   Yowie
Height   About 1.5 metres
Habitat Eastern Australia
Status   UNEXPLAINED

Strange footprints in the sand? Unexplained attacks on pets and other animals? Watch out – there could be a Yowie about!

HAIRY HORRORS

When settlers first came to Australia in the 1800s, Aboriginal people had already lived there for thousands of years. The Aborigines were great story-tellers and often spoke of fierce ape-like creatures called **Yowies**. They thought Yowies lurked in lonely parts of the **bush** and came out at night in search of prey.

At first, the settlers were doubtful – but it was not long before they started to think the stories might be true. Over the next century, countless people all over Australia claimed to find large footprints or see hairy, gorilla-like creatures walking upright in the forests and mountains.

This wooden statue of a Yowie is in Queensland, Australia. People who claim to have seen Yowies say they look either like large monkeys or ape-like human beings.

CLOSE ENCOUNTER

One person who is convinced that Yowies exist is Australian cryptid hunter Rex Gilroy. After his own close encounter with a Yowie one night in 1970, Gilroy started to collect evidence and analyze the sightings.

Gilroy's theory is that Yowies belong to an extinct type of ape. Others argue that the original Yowies were not apes at all, but Aboriginal people who were driven out of their tribe for committing crimes and who lived far away from everybody else in the **outback**.

FACT OR FAKE?

In the 1970s many people in Australia reported seeing Yowies, but proof has always been hard to find. Recently Yowies have been blamed for attacks on household pets, but these are more likely the work of wild animals, such as **dingoes**.

Australian cryptid hunter Rex Gilroy displays a cast said to have been made from a Yowie footprint.

The Australian outback is a vast desert area of dry grasslands and forests. There is certainly enough space for a population of apes here, but what would they live on?

Who analyzed evidence of Yowie sightings?

What species is the Yowie said to belong to?

What other theory might explain the Yowie?

THE MAROZI

Walking alone in the African bush, you find yourself face to face with a fierce creature that has terrifying teeth and razor-sharp claws. But is it a lion, a leopard – or a Marozi?

Marozi are small lions that have leopard-like markings. Similar animals have been bred in captivity, but they are rarely seen in the wild.

LION OR LEOPARD?

In 1923, a British hunter was crossing the Aberdare mountains near Mount Kinangop in Kenya, when he saw what he thought were two unusual-coloured leopards. His guides told him they were mountain lions, known locally as Marozi. He later inspected the tracks, which were more like those of a lion than a leopard. Normally, lions do not live in woodland or in the mountains, but on open grassy plains.

CRYPTID FILE

Name Marozi
Size About 1.8 metres long, excluding tail
Habitat Kenya, East Africa
Status UNEXPLAINED

What two animals does the Marozi most resemble?

Where was a Marozi seen in 1923?

Who went in search of the Marozi in 1933?

THE ABERDARE LIONS

Twelve years years later, a Kenyan farmer shot two similar creatures in a forest in the Aberdare Mountains. He sent the skins to the capital, Nairobi, for study. The 'Aberdare Lions' were found to be an adult male and female. They were slightly smaller than most lions, and had spots on the sides of their bodies and a dark stripe along their back.

WHAT HAPPENEND NEXT?

In 1933, the English adventurer Kenneth Dower organized an expedition into the hill forests to find the Marozi. He heard lots of stories, but failed to capture a Marozi alive. Sightings of the Marozi continued to be made until the 1970s. Perhaps after that, the animals became extinct.

FACT OR FAKE?

Some say the Marozi is a cross between a lion and a leopard. Others think that it is a type of lion that has somehow kept its baby spots into adulthood. Some scientists think that the Marozi belongs to a separate species of lion found only in mountain regions.

How many of the cryptids in this book really exist? We may never know. But there are certainly many more animals still out there, waiting to be discovered!

KNOWN ANIMALS...

Often, cryptids turn out not to exist, or just to be different versions of animals that are already known. But once in a while an entirely new type of animal is discovered.

CRYPTID FILE

Subject	Okapi
Height	1.5 to 2 metres
Habitat	Ituri Rainforest, central Africa
Status	RECOGNIZED SPECIES

... AND NEW SPECIES

The okapi (*oh-kah-pee*) was recognized in 1901. The coelacanth (*see-lo-canth*) was identified in 1938. The Yemen monitor lizard was identified in 1991. In each case, people in the area had been talking about the animal for years, but scientists refused to believe it existed.

 Okapi are members of the giraffe family and live in the Ituri rainforest of central Africa. They were unknown to western scientists until an explorer captured one for study in 1901.

THE SAOLA

For centuries, the saola, a type of small antelope, lived undetected in the forest regions of eastern Indochina. Then in 1991, a hunter found a saola skull in the mountains and showed it to a scientist. A team of experts visited the region, saw the saola, photographed it and captured it for study. Even now, the creatures are very rare, and only 11 have been officially sighted.

The saola is one of the world's rarest mammals. Local people call it the 'polite animal' because it moves so quietly through the forest.

THE COELACANTH

The huge deep sea fish known as the coelacanth was thought to have vanished with the dinosaurs 65 million years ago. The first living specimen was found off the east African coast in 1938. A second species was discovered in Indonesia in 1998.

When was the okapi accepted as a real animal?

Where does the saola live?

When was the first living coelacanth discovered?

A scientist examines a coelacanth caught by Kenyan fishermen in April 2001.

GLOSSARY

Aboriginal Original tribal inhabitant of Australia.

Adapt To change in order to suit your surroundings or way of life.

Amphibious Able to live both on land and in water.

Bigfoot An ape-like creature said to live in the forests of the northwest USA.

Bunyip A seal-like creature said to live in the Australian outback.

Bush An area of wilderness in Australia.

Creek A narrow valley with water running through it.

Crow's nest A platform at the top of a ship's mast where a lookout keeps watch.

Cryptid A creature that does not belong to a known species.

Cryptozoologist A person who studies cryptids.

Dingo A type of wild dog native to Australia.

Evolution A process by which species gradually change and adapt over time.

Expedition A mission to explore a place or area.

Ferocious Fierce and aggressive.

Folklore Songs, stories and dances that are handed down from one generation to the next.

Laboratory Place where scientists carry out tests and experiments.

Lagoon A type of lake.

Legend A story that has been told many times, but may or may not be true.

Loch A Scottish name for a deep lake.

Marsupial A creature that carries its young in a pouch, such as a kangaroo.

Missionary A person who travels from place to place in order to tell people about a religion.

Monastery A place where monks live.

Myth An ancient story that is often found not to be true.

Naturalist A person who studies the natural world.

Outback A remote area of wilderness in Australia.

Plesiosaur A type of prehistoric sea creature.

Prehistoric Very ancient, dating back to the time before writing and record-keeping were invented.

Sasquatch Native American name for **Bigfoot**.

Scalp Skin and hair covering the top and back of the head.

Scrubland An area of low-growing bushes and trees.

Settler A person who moves to another country to start a new life.

Sloth A slow-moving tropical creature that lives in trees.

Species A group of creatures, animals or plants.

Superstition Something that is believed to be true, but has no basis in fact.

Wombat A four-legged animal found in Australia.

Yeti A large ape-like creature said to live in the mountains of Nepal.

Yowie A hairy ape-like creature said to live in the Australian bush.

ANSWERS

Page

8-9   Sasquatch; 220 kilograms; Roger Patterson and Robert Gimlin.

10-11   From the Aborigines; in lakes and lagoons; on the banks of the Murrumbidgee River in New South Wales.

12-13   Hans Egede; off the coast of Greenland; 20 metres.

14-15   Ramón Lista; about 2.5 metres; Vernon Hesketh-Prichard.

16-17   Scotland; George Spicer and his wife; 2003.

18-19   Up to 20 metres long; from a Native American song; Lake Okanagan.

20-1   About 1 metre; central Sumatran jungle; Debbie Martyr.

22-3   Congo River basin, central Africa; 'one who stops rivers'; Ivan Sanderson.

24-5   Rex Gilroy; ape; Yowies could be members of Aboriginal tribes who were driven out for committing crimes.

26-7   A lion and a leopard; near Mount Kinangop in the Aberdare mountains of Kenya; the English adventurer Kenneth Dower.

28-9   1901; forest regions of Indochina; 1938.

WEBSITES

INDEX